Dogs are popular over the world. company, they c commands and can act trained guide dogs help around. No wonder dogs have earned the title of 'man's best friend'. Dogs come in all shapes and sizes, and they need a lot of looking after. As well as food, drink and shelter, they need plenty of exercise.

Today, many dog-owners expect their pets to be as well looked after medically as themselves. Dogs and cats make up the vast majority of patients for small veterinary practices.

When you throw a stick, your dog will run to bring it back to you. This is a good form of exercise and training.

FACT BOX
Dogs' bones have been found at prehistoric campsites. The earliest cave-dwellers probably found dogs useful as guards and hunting companions. The first dogs to make friends with people were probably more like modern-day wolves.

AT THE VETS

To become a qualified veterinary surgeon, you have to take a degree course at a veterinary college. These courses are very popular, and you have to pass certain exams at school to get a place. Science subjects, such as biology and chemistry, are important. Training at college lasts several years. Most new vets start as assistants in a veterinary practice.

Vets use many of the same medical instruments as human doctors. A stethoscope helps them listen to their patients' heartbeat and breathing.

Like many small animals, puppies are full of energy and curiosity. The vet may need help to keep the puppies on the examination table!

Even healthy puppies have worms at some time. Owners need to visit a vet if their puppy coughs, eats poorly, has a high temperature or generally seems unwell.

Wannabe...

A Vet

Neil Morris

· PARRAGON ·

LOOKING AFTER ANIMALS

Anyone who wants to become a vet has to like being with animals and looking after them. Vet stands for veterinary surgeon, which means animal doctor. Veterinary surgeons are called veterinarians in the USA and some other countries. If you have pets at home, you are probably used to caring for animals.

To give rabbits a supply of water, a feeding bottle can be hung from the side of their hutch.

Cats are favourite pets. Vets sometimes call them 'companion animals', because people have pets to keep them company.

Rabbits are usually kept in a hutch. If you are thinking of having a rabbit or any other pet, remember that they need looking after all the time, not just when it suits you!

Veterinary nurses help vets in their work.

Veterinary nurses help vets in their work. Students must have two years' experience at a training centre before they become qualified veterinary nurses. As in human hospitals and doctors' surgeries, veterinary surgeons and nurses work as a team. In general practice, pets are brought in for health checks and treatment. As well as surgeons and nurses, the practice may have assistants, trainees and receptionists.

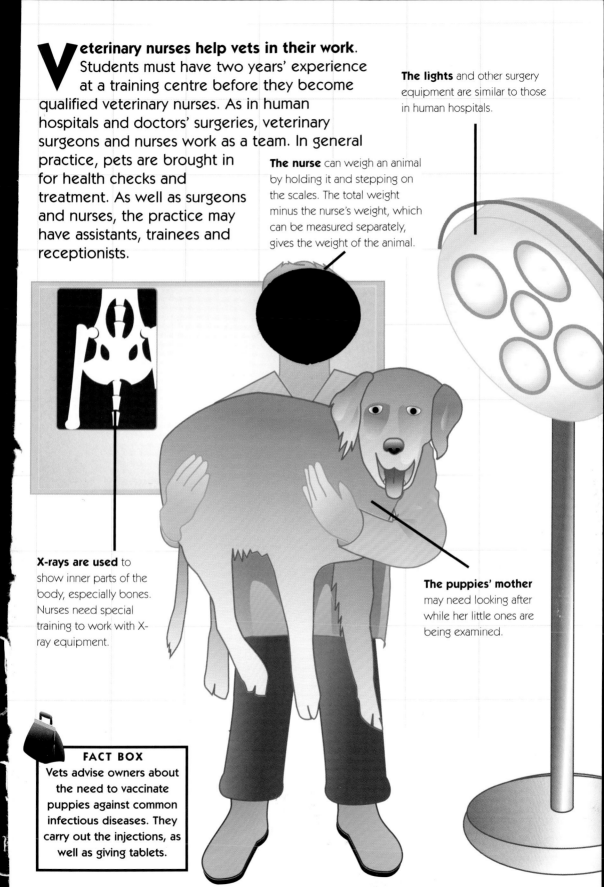

The lights and other surgery equipment are similar to those in human hospitals.

The nurse can weigh an animal by holding it and stepping on the scales. The total weight minus the nurse's weight, which can be measured separately, gives the weight of the animal.

X-rays are used to show inner parts of the body, especially bones. Nurses need special training to work with X-ray equipment.

The puppies' mother may need looking after while her little ones are being examined.

FACT BOX
Vets advise owners about the need to vaccinate puppies against common infectious diseases. They carry out the injections, as well as giving tablets.

ON THE FARM

Country vets spend much of their time **working** with local farm animals. Today, horses are generally kept as 'companions' rather than as working animals. They may be ponies, kept as pets and for riding, or even showjumpers or racehorses. These animals are extremely valuable to their owners, who want to make sure that they stay healthy.

Vets check horses' teeth regularly. They also inject healthy horses to protect them against illnesses such as tetanus and influenza.

Many veterinary students want to train to be an equine vet, which means a 'horse doctor'. But you must qualify as a general vet first, before specializing in horses.

Just like a doctor, a travelling vet needs to have his bag of drugs and equipment with him at all times.

FACT BOX
In 1769-70 an English racehorse called Eclipse won every single race it ran. When the horse died, its body was examined by a famous French veterinary scientist, Vial de St Bel. The French expert then stayed on to found the Royal Veterinary College in London.

Most farm animals are so-called 'food animals', which farmers keep for their milk, eggs and meat. Farmers want to look after their animals well, but at the same time they are running a business. Vets advise farmers on feeding and welfare, as well as on their animals' health. Sometimes there are widespread problems affecting whole groups of animals in a region, and vets must deal with these quickly and effectively.

Baby pigs are sensitive to cold temperatures, and must be kept warm just after they are born. Piglets are fed as much as they will eat so that they gain weight quickly.

Dairy cattle, such as Jersey cows, are kept for the milk they produce. Beef cattle, such as Herefords, are reared to produce meat.

Free-range cockerels, hens and chicks are allowed to move about the farm.

LAMBING TIME

Springtime is a very busy season for country vets. Ewes, or female sheep, give birth to one or two lambs, usually in the spring. This is lambing time. Farmers and vets need to keep a watch on flocks of sheep, in case there are problems for either mother or young. Experienced farmers know when there might be a difficult birth and call the vet well in time. Or there might be an emergency. Being a vet is a 24-hour job, and you must always be ready to help.

FACT BOX
People started keeping wild sheep thousands of years ago, probably in Asia. Today there are over 400 breeds of domestic sheep, and there are still wild sheep in some parts of the world.

Farmers and vets have to make sure that all newly-born animals can breathe properly at once. They may have to clear a lamb's nostrils and mouth.

Sometimes ewes ignore their young and do nothing to look after them. The farmer and the vet must be ready to act quickly to help any abandoned lambs.

In most domestic breeds of sheep, the ewes have no horns. The males of domestic and wild sheep, called rams, usually do grow horns.

Country vets often have a lot of travelling to do. They may have to find remote farms in a hurry, so they must be able to drive. Preferably they need a vehicle that they can drive along muddy lanes and even across fields.

Four-wheel drive vehicles are perfect for farm conditions. They are also spacious enough to transport sick animals.

ANIMAL RESCUE

Veterinary specialists also work in many fields of wildlife conservation. Animal welfare societies and rescue organizations care for injured animals, and vets may be called in to help. Unfortunately there are sometimes major catastrophes, such as oil spills, that endanger large groups of wildlife. Seabirds cannot survive oil without help.

If its feathers are clogged with oil, a bird cannot fly or swim properly. It quickly loses body heat

Protective, hard-wearing clothing is needed for most animal rescue work.

Oiled birds preen their feathers to try and get rid of the oil, but this means that they take in the oil and quickly make themselves ill.

Oil slicks have polluted many of our coasts. Today's oil tankers are so huge that there is always a risk of a vast spillage if they run into trouble.

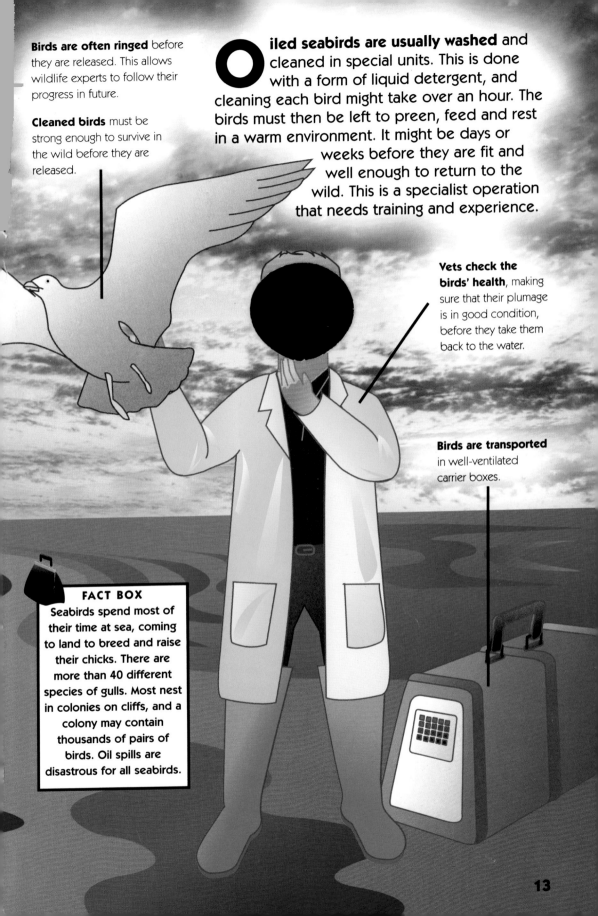

Birds are often ringed before they are released. This allows wildlife experts to follow their progress in future.

Cleaned birds must be strong enough to survive in the wild before they are released.

Oiled seabirds are usually washed and cleaned in special units. This is done with a form of liquid detergent, and cleaning each bird might take over an hour. The birds must then be left to preen, feed and rest in a warm environment. It might be days or weeks before they are fit and well enough to return to the wild. This is a specialist operation that needs training and experience.

Vets check the birds' health, making sure that their plumage is in good condition, before they take them back to the water.

Birds are transported in well-ventilated carrier boxes.

FACT BOX
Seabirds spend most of their time at sea, coming to land to breed and raise their chicks. There are more than 40 different species of gulls. Most nest in colonies on cliffs, and a colony may contain thousands of pairs of birds. Oil spills are disastrous for all seabirds.

MARINE WORLD

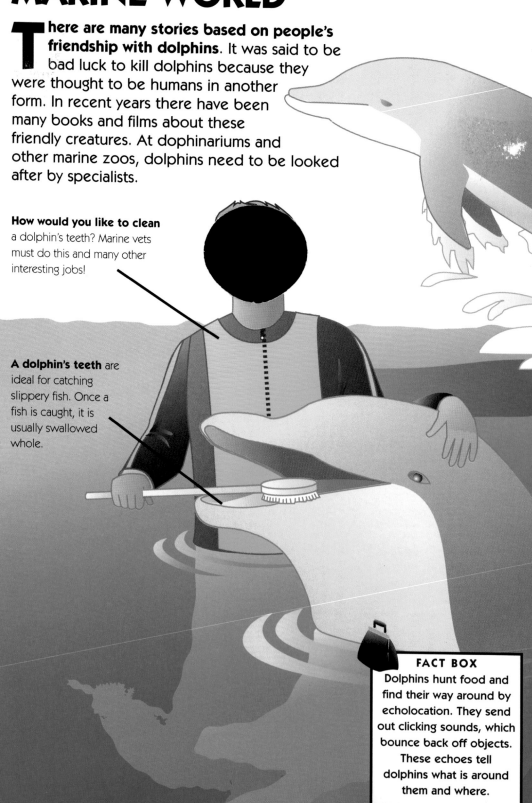

There are many stories based on people's friendship with dolphins. It was said to be bad luck to kill dolphins because they were thought to be humans in another form. In recent years there have been many books and films about these friendly creatures. At dolphinariums and other marine zoos, dolphins need to be looked after by specialists.

How would you like to clean a dolphin's teeth? Marine vets must do this and many other interesting jobs!

A dolphin's teeth are ideal for catching slippery fish. Once a fish is caught, it is usually swallowed whole.

FACT BOX
Dolphins hunt food and find their way around by echolocation. They send out clicking sounds, which bounce back off objects. These echoes tell dolphins what is around them and where.

Dolphins seem to enjoy leaping through the air. The record for the highest dolphin jump stands at well over 4 metres!

Watching dolphins in the wild, and in large tanks in dolphinariums, has told wildlife experts a lot about their behaviour. Dolphins have large brains compared with other mammals, and they have a great ability to learn. They appear to enjoy performing tricks in captivity. Some people feel it is wrong to take them from the wild, while others argue that it is a good way of learning more about them. Whatever they believe, vets and other specialists make sure that the dolphins are well looked after.

This vet is checking the dolphin's blowhole. Dolphins come to the surface regularly to breathe in fresh air.

FACT BOX
Dolphins sometimes get stranded on beaches. Vets help to reduce the beached animal's stress by keeping it cool and wet, until it can be moved back out to sea.

AT THE ZOO

Years ago **zoological gardens**, or zoos, were places where wild animals were kept in cramped cages for the so-called amusement of visitors. Today's zoos are much more animal-friendly, and they are useful for research as well as entertainment. Zoo vets keep the animals well, treating them when they are sick and operating on them if necessary.

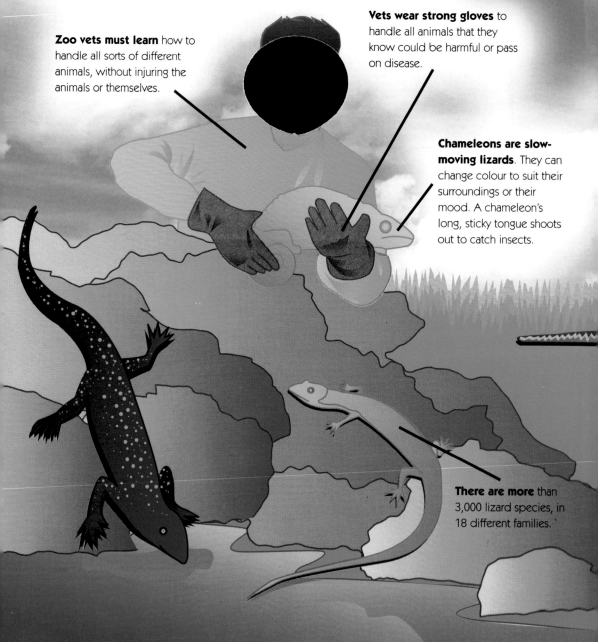

Zoo vets must learn how to handle all sorts of different animals, without injuring the animals or themselves.

Vets wear strong gloves to handle all animals that they know could be harmful or pass on disease.

Chameleons are slow-moving lizards. They can change colour to suit their surroundings or their mood. A chameleon's long, sticky tongue shoots out to catch insects.

There are more than 3,000 lizard species, in 18 different families.

Tree-climbing snakes first wrap their tail around a branch. Then they stretch out the front of their body and hook their neck around the tree farther up.

Specialist vets recommend diets to zoo-keepers, and supervise preparation of the animals' food. Most zoos have an animal hospital, as well as a laboratory where scientific studies of diseases can be carried out. There are also a variety of jobs for veterinary nurses in zoos.

Snakes move by using large scales on the underside of their belly to pull them forward.

Would you like to learn to handle snakes safely and properly? In the reptile house, keepers know which of the snakes are poisonous and how to make sure they are not bitten.

WILDLIFE RESERVE

In most countries of the world, areas have been set aside to protect wild animals and plants. In these national parks and wildlife reserves, wardens make sure that people obey the local laws, while vets look after the medical needs of the animals. There are many reserves in Africa, and large numbers of tourists go there each year on safari holidays. This brings in a lot of money and helps African countries protect their animals.

Sometimes vets fit radio collars to wild animals. This allows them to keep track of the animals and study their range.

Jeeps are perfect for the African grasslands. If vets or wardens need to take an animal to hospital, they bring in a larger vehicle.

Expert wildlife vets tranquillize animals quite safely. When the rhino wakes up, it just carries on as if nothing had happened.

FACT BOX

Both the black and white rhinoceroses of Africa are actually coloured grey. Both have two horns on their forehead, a long one at the front and a smaller one behind. They stand about 1.8 metres tall and measure up to 5 metres from head to tail.

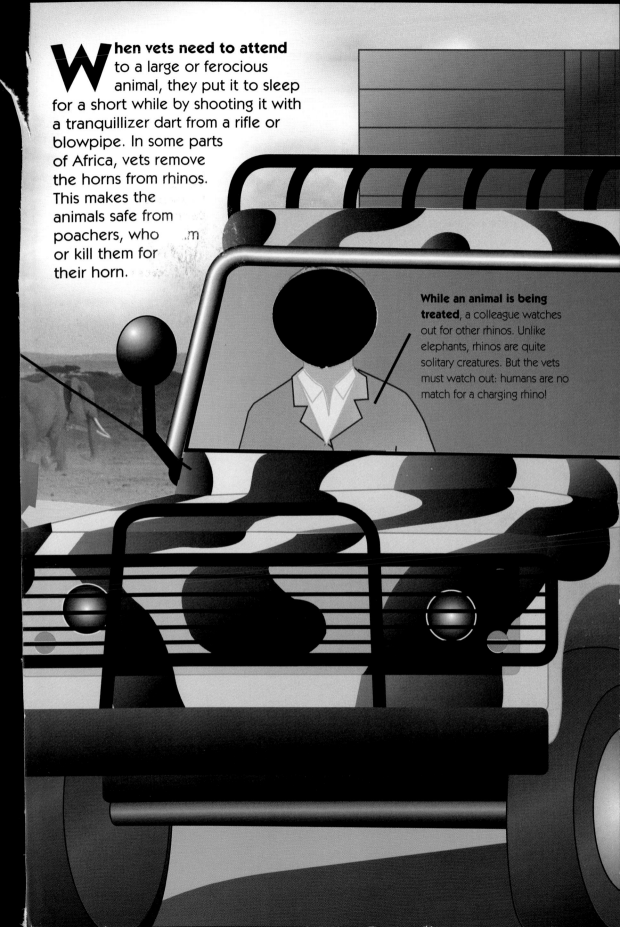

When vets need to attend to a large or ferocious animal, they put it to sleep for a short while by shooting it with a tranquillizer dart from a rifle or blowpipe. In some parts of Africa, vets remove the horns from rhinos. This makes the animals safe from poachers, who ...m or kill them for their horn.

While an animal is being treated, a colleague watches out for other rhinos. Unlike elephants, rhinos are quite solitary creatures. But the vets must watch out: humans are no match for a charging rhino!

FROM PAST TO FUTURE

What sort of work will vets of the future do? Much of it will probably be similar to today, but future veterinary scientists might do much more research in genetics. This is the study of heredity and the way in which characteristics are passed on from animal to animal. Perhaps it will one day be possible to produce living beings from the genes of long-dead animals.

Triceratops was a horned and armoured dinosaur that lived about 72 million years ago. Its name means 'three-horned face'. Although it was a plant-eater rather than a meat-eater, Triceratops could do a lot of damage on the run. It weighed over 5 tonnes.

Maybe vets of the future will look after cats and dogs, too – as well as being chased by previously extinct reptiles!

FACT BOX
Is it right for scientists to try and change animals' and plants' genetic make-up with drugs? Many people feel that we need strong regulations to stop this so-called genetic engineering.

Dinosaurs died out 65 million years ago, long before humans walked on Earth. But perhaps in future scientists will be able to use fossil genes to bring them to life again! But where would the dinosaurs live, and what would happen if they started to run wild? Vets and other experts of the future may be able to answer these questions.

Just like today, vets of the future will want to study animals and their behaviour close-up. This might be rather difficult with dinosaurs!

In many of today's wildlife reserves wild animals are watched from high towers. It might be safer for both humans and animals if this happened in future too.

FACT BOX
Like doctors, vets swear an oath. They promise to try always to ensure the welfare of animals in their care. Vets will surely continue to keep this promise in future.